Sleeper's Awake!

Book 2 - Student Level

To my son

Shawn Davidson

Foreword

Hymns, including Greek and Latin, the psalter or book of psalms, ancient chant, early canticles, spirituals, and contemporary gospel, have created a hymnody, which over many centuries has become the most profound vehicle for praise and worship in the Christian Church. It has once been said that the Church, "Has come singing down through the ages". Through this beautiful medium of song, worshippers over many generations have privately and collectively aspired to give praise and proclaim their faith while expressing the higher emotions of the soul.

My dear son, Christian Davidson, who was himself a composer and arranger, had a particular fondness for the works of JS Bach, and in particular, Cantata number 140. This Cantata was based on a hymn written in 1598 by Philipp Nicolai named Sleeper's Awake! Four hundred and twenty years later, and through Christian's inspiration, this book was to be produced and derive its name.

After several months during 2006 twenty hymn arrangements were all but completed. However, the project stalled for a decade until, almost to the day, a new student would be the encouragement and grace to motivate me to revisit the project. I thank Terry-Lynn Mireault for her timely and spiritual support in the production of Sleeper's Awake!

These twenty arrangements were carefully written with much consideration given to the original four-part choral arrangements found in several of the well known hymn books. Some of these arrangements were based on personal tastes and compositional ideas. As the arrangements in Book 1 would challenge many of the seasoned players, a second book of the same hymns is arranged at a more moderate level for students. Book 3 follows in line with twenty duets for voice and guitar.

It is my desire that as many guitarists as possible may enjoy the beauty and peace of these wonderful melodies.

I wish to thank Ben Robertson for his assistance as editorial advisor. I also wish to express my gratitude to Rowland Marshall for his artwork and quote. And I particularly would like to thank Donna Moore for her beautiful cover design.

Kenneth Michael Davidson
March 2018

Index of Hymns

Abide With Me

Henry F. Lyte - William H. Monk

Holy, Holy, Holy

Reginald Heber - John B. Dykes
1783 - 1826   1861

Immortal, Invisible,
God Only Wise

Walter C. Smith 1867

In The Garden

C. Austin Miles

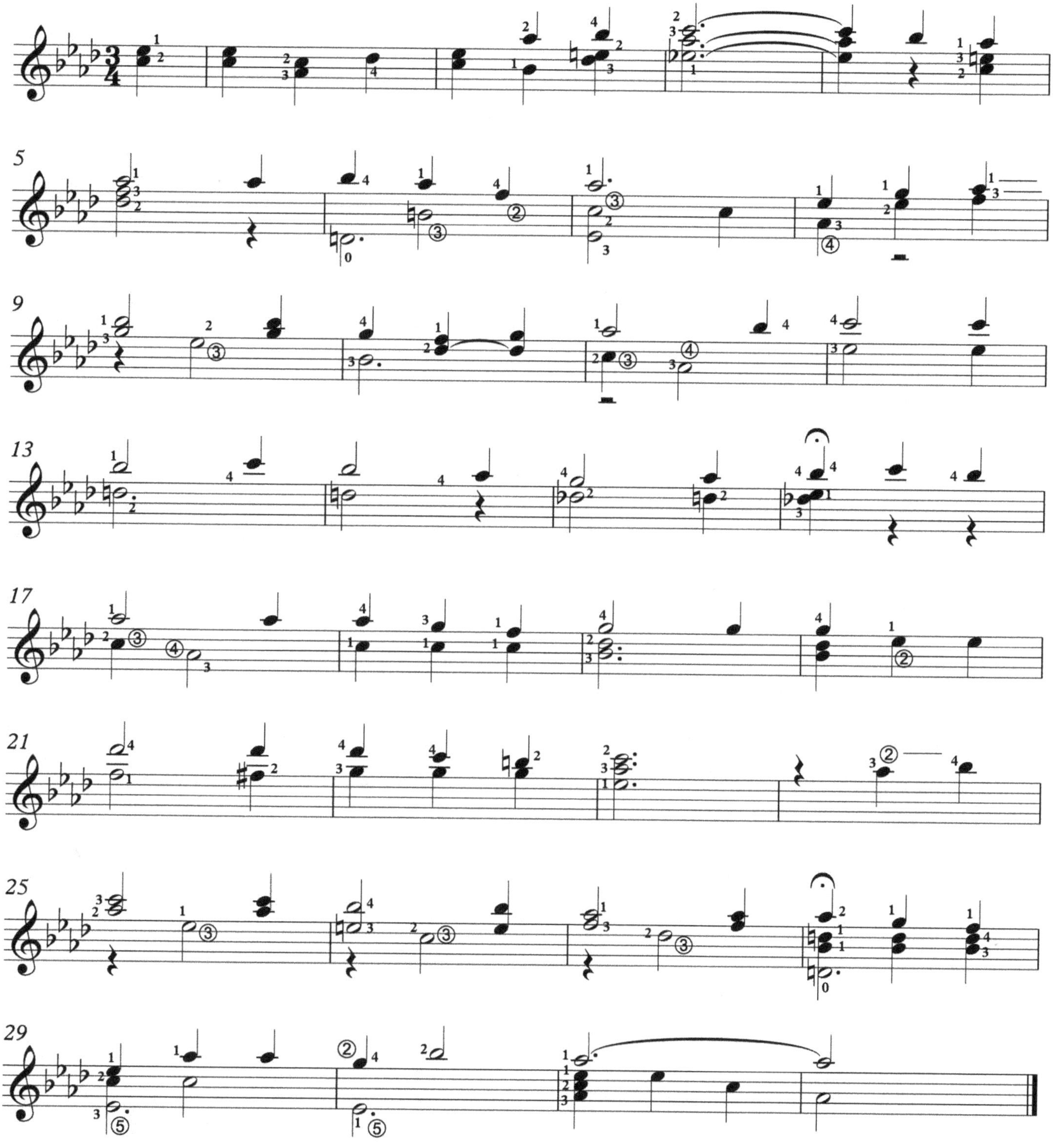

Shall We Gather At The River

Robert Lowry

The Lord Is My Shepherd

From Psalm 23 - Jesse Seymour Irvine

Thine Be The Glory

George Frederick Handel

The Old Rugged Cross

George Bennard

Infant Holy, Infant Lowly

Polish Carol - W. Zlobie Lezy - E. M. G. Reed 1933

Rejoice, The Lord Is King

Charles Wesley 1746 - John Darwall 1779

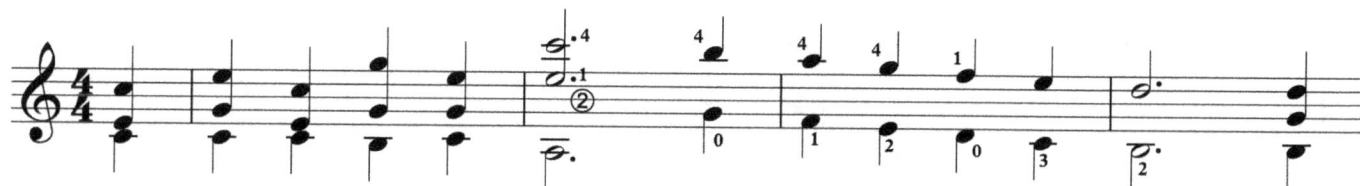

We Gather Together

Netherlands Folk Song

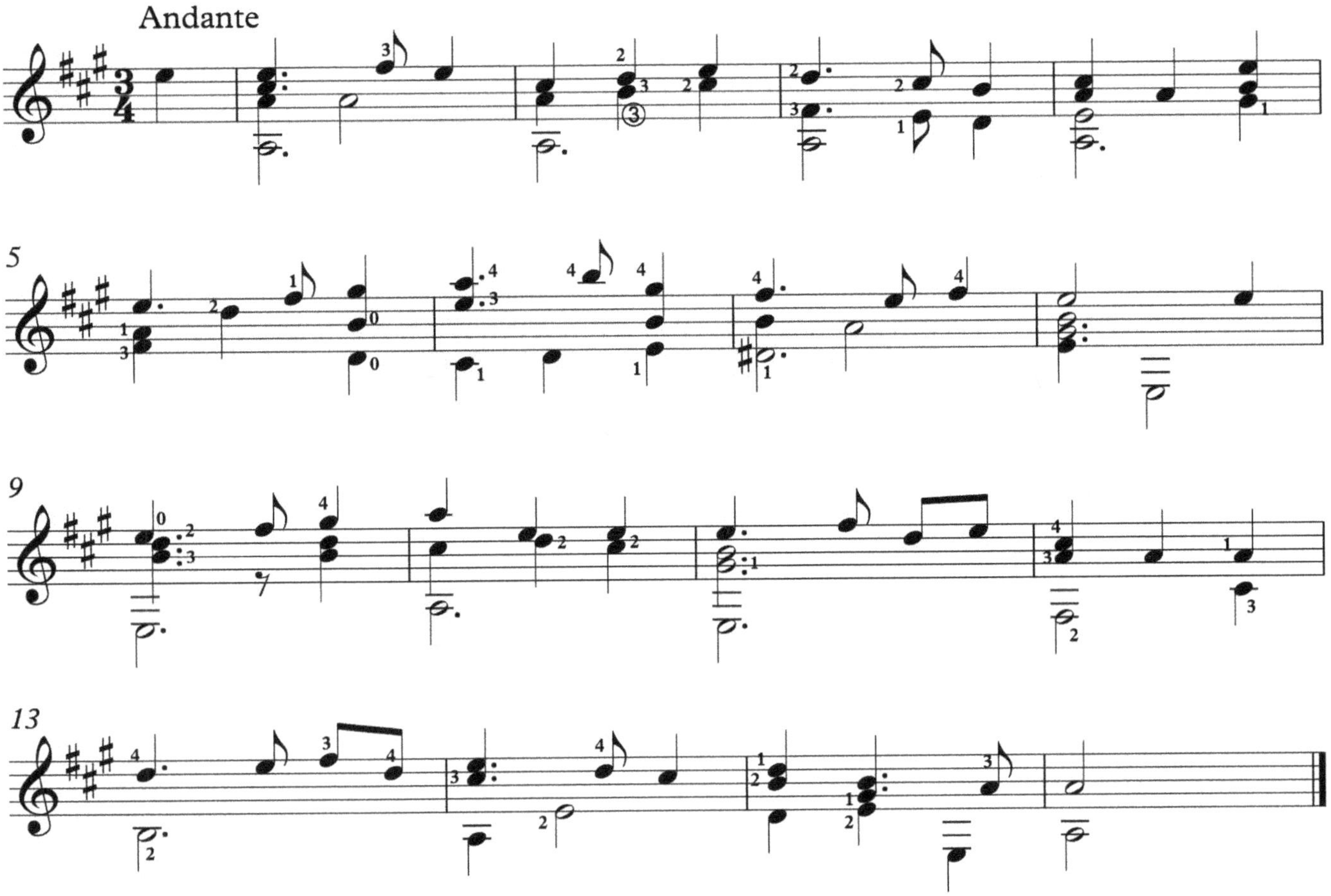

Blessed Assurance

Fanny J. Crosby - Phoebe P. Knapp

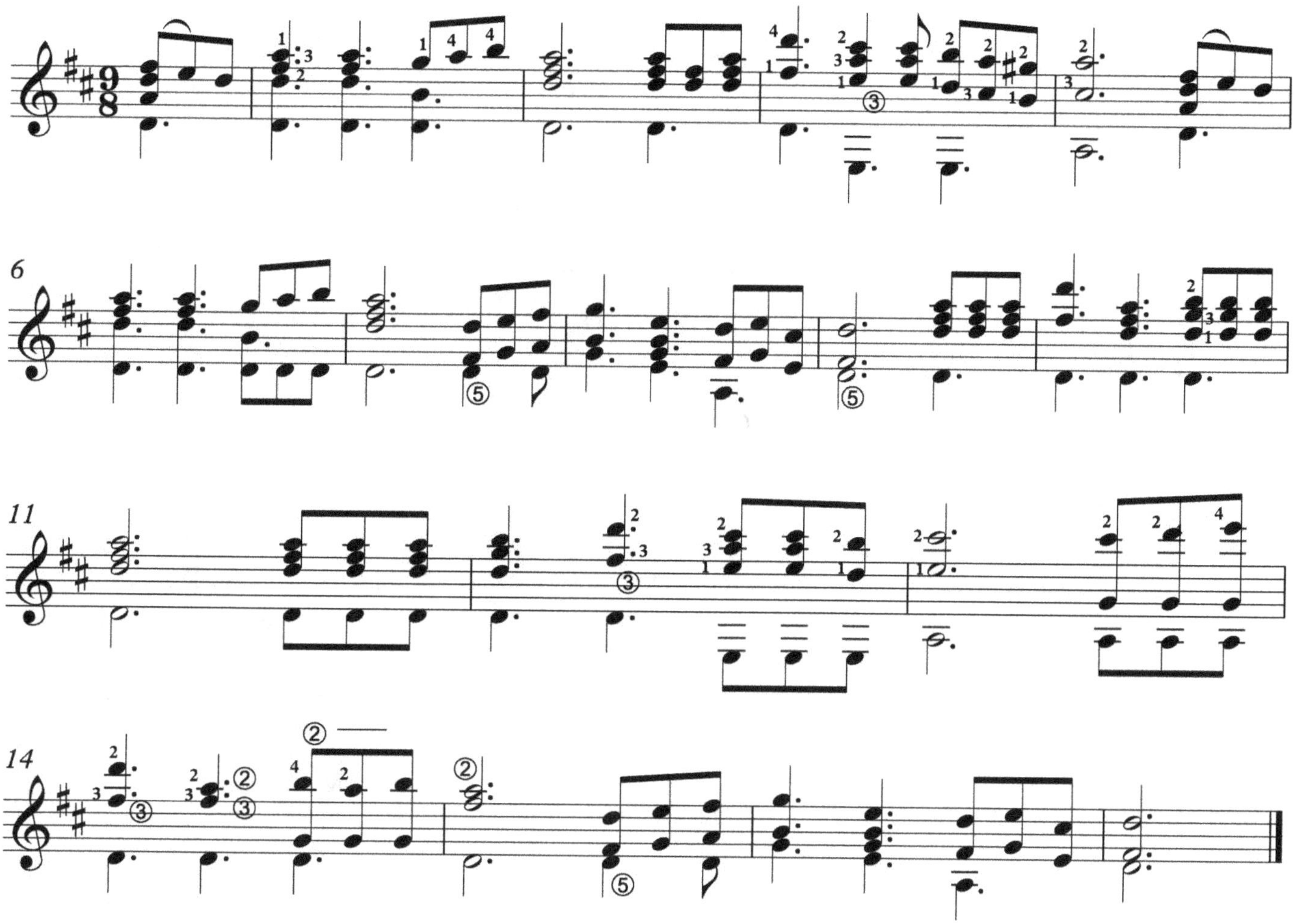

All For Jesus

Mary D. James - Asa Hull

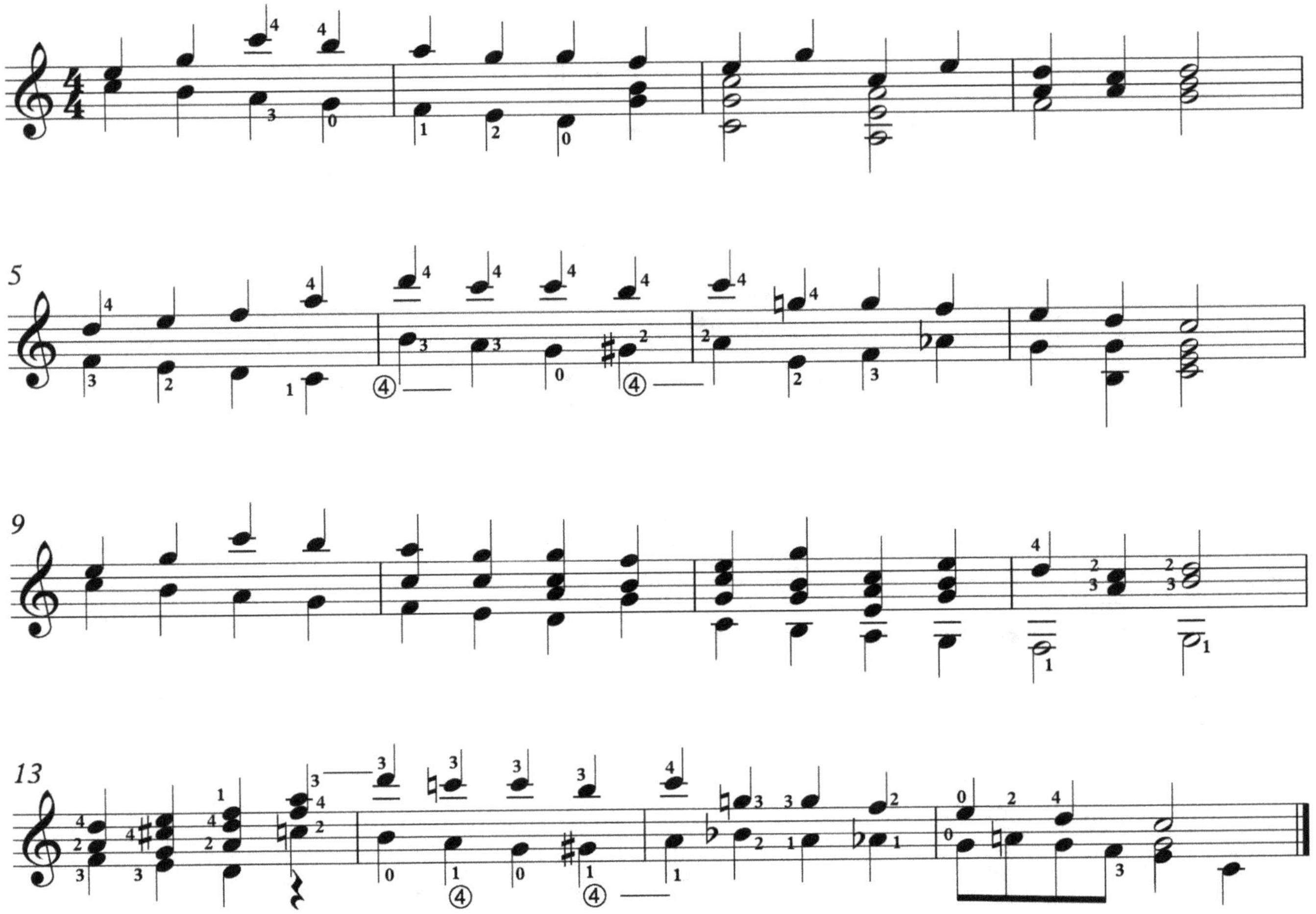

He Leadeth Me: O Blessed Thought

Joseph H. Gilmore 1862 - William B. Bradbury 1864

Jesus, Thou Joy Of Loving Hearts

Music: Henry Baker - 1854 - Words: Bernard of Clairvaux, 12th Century

Amazing Grace

John Newton

Alleluia! Sing To Jesus

William C. Dix 1866 - Rowland H. Prichard 1830

This Is My Father's World

Traditional English Melody

Easter Hymn

Charles Wesley 1739 - Lyra Davidica 1708

Wachet auf, uns die Stimme

(Sleepers Awake)Philipp Nicolai 1598
Chorale from Cantata No. 140 - Johann Sebastian Bach

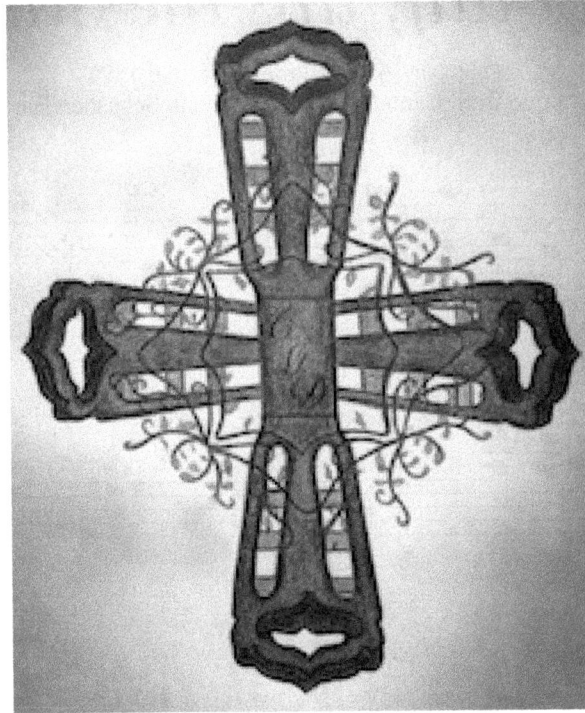

Published in Canada by Kenneth Michael Davidson
Nova Scotia, Canada
macdhaimusic@gmail.com

Library and Archives Canada Cataloguing in Publication
ISBN 978-0-9958107-5-4

Acknowledgments

Christian Davidson	His Inspiration and Title of this Book
Ben Robertson	Music Editorial Advisor
Terry-Lynn Mireault	Spiritual Consultant
Biography Photo	Linda Canton
Donna Moore	Front Cover Art and Design
Rowland C. Marshall	Back Cover Artwork Insert and Quote

www.ingramcontent.com/pod-product-compliance
Lightning Source LLC
Chambersburg PA
CBHW080939040426

42443CB00015B/3482